Designs
for
Pyrography
and
Other Crafts

Designs
for
Pyrography
and
Other Crafts

Norma Gregory

GUILD OF MASTER CRAFTSMAN PUBLICATIONS

Guild of Master Craftsman Publications Ltd
166 High Street, Lewes
East Sussex BN7 1XU

Reprinted 2004

ISBN 1 86108 320 3

British Cataloguing in Publication Data
A catalogue record of this book is available from the British Library.

Publisher: Paul Richardson
Art Director: Ian Smith
Production Manager: Stuart Poole
Managing Editor: Gerrie Purcell
Commissioning Editor: April McCroskie
Editor: Gill Parris
Designer: Danny McBride
Cover and Gallery Photographs: Anthony Bailey
Photographs on pp. 5, 7, 8, 9 and 10: Paul Leavan, Artography
Diagrams and illustrations: Norma Gregory

Typeface: Champers, Neuzeit Gro, Futura

Colour origination by Rare Repro Ltd

Printed and Bound by Kyodo Printing Co. Pte Ltd, Singapore

For my sons David and Peter, with love.

Acknowledgements

All my life I have drawn, painted and made things, encouraged by my mother and by some exceptional and inspirational teachers. To them my thanks for filling my life with enjoyment and adventure.

Thanks are also due to my husband Dennis and to friends and students for their encouragement, and to the large number of people who have contacted me from around the world after using the designs from my first book. To the editorial staff at the Guild of Master Craftsman Publications, my grateful thanks for their help in the compilation of this book.

Contents

Introduction

One of the main problems I have encountered over the years has been the lack of suitable design sources for people who have difficulty in drawing their own. As a result of this, my first book, *Pyrography Designs,* was published by GMC Publications in 1999. This appealed to a wide range of workers in different crafts and has proved to be a bestseller at home and abroad.

This book contains new designs, but follows the same flexible approach to their use that I introduced in my first book so, by extracting different elements such as flower buds, leaves or bows from various designs, you can create your own unique design.

If you want to use the designs for miniature work then you will have to reduce them accordingly (see page 8). The majority of the designs are suitable for most kinds of crafts, including greetings cards, bookmarks, gift tags, boxes, fingerplates and many more that I am sure you will think of yourself. Remember, if you are working on boxes, that they also have sides and a front as well as a top!

Most available designs provide you with outlines only. They do not usually show you where to put shading, which is essential if you want to give your work realism and depth. Because of this, I have added shading to the designs, to suggest where it should go but, if you wish, you can change this to suit your own idea of how you want the finished article to look.

Colour can, of course, be added to any of these designs, but do be careful to choose the right type of paint for your finished work, depending on what and where it is going to be used. Choose the colours you use carefully, and try to keep them within their natural range.

Most of all, enjoy creating something different and personal. I hope the designs will inspire you. If they do, you may wish to look at the first book of designs, as this contains sections on sea life, fungi, box designs and different flower, animal and bird designs.

Chapter

1

How to Use the Designs

Adapting the designs

Here are a few hints, which will help you to achieve the most out of the designs on pp. 16-99.

• Check that your chosen design will fit the shape you are working on. Try to avoid large empty areas that can make the design look unbalanced, or as if something is missing.

Example of poor balance. The motif is too near the top edge of the card.

Better position of the motif, and the shape of the card is used to better effect.

• Note the perspective. In general objects become smaller as they get further away from you, so be careful, when adapting the designs, to avoid elements in the background larger than they should be in relation to those in the foreground.

The beehive is out of proportion with the gate. As it is further away, it should be smaller than the gate.

The beehive is reduced in size to fit behind the gate, thus obeying the laws of perspective.

• Fix where your source of light is coming from and make a note of this. If the light is coming from the left-hand side, then all the shadows will be going towards the right, and vice versa.

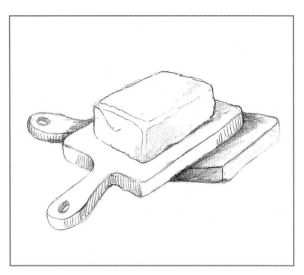

Butter on butter pats

• Remember that light and shade are important to your work, whatever medium you use, as they bring life, form and movement and make it look much more natural.

• The designs in this book are drawn so that you can adapt them. You may need a longer stem on a flower, for example, or a longer extension in the middle of a border design; with this in mind, I have only drawn short stems, and have left gaps in the centre of border designs so that you can extend the stalks to suit your own composition.

• When you are using one of the animal or bird designs, you may find that they will look more natural if you trace them with a dotted outline, rather than a solid one.

Nearly all these designs can be adapted to suit your needs. It is really up to you to be as creative and as adventurous with them as you wish. For example, you can take one or more motifs from a design to create a new one; put one or more complete designs together to produce a new one of your own; or combine lots of smaller elements to be even more creative.

To make up a composite design, select the images you want to use and trace them onto separate pieces of tracing paper that are slightly larger than the design that you are tracing. Next, place all the tracings you need on a sheet of plain paper and treat them like jigsaw pieces, moving and re-arranging them until you have a pleasing, well-balanced design. When you are happy with the arrangement, use tiny pieces of low-tack masking tape, and carefully stick them down onto the white paper.

Combining separate elements to make a new, composite design, is much like putting together the pieces of a jigsaw.

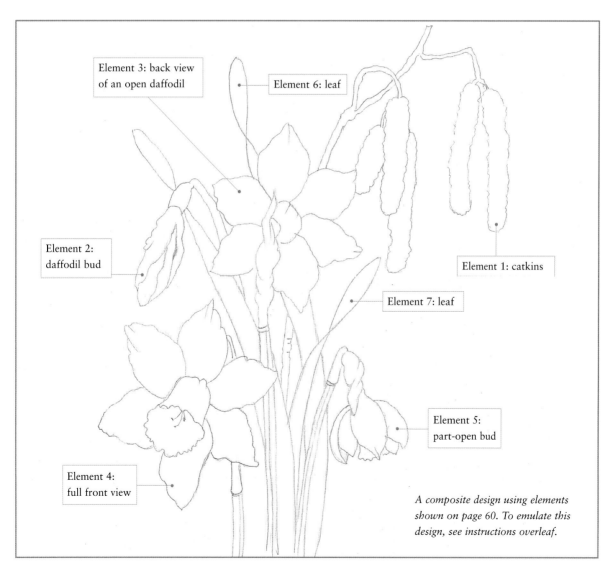

Element 3: back view of an open daffodil

Element 6: leaf

Element 2: daffodil bud

Element 1: catkins

Element 7: leaf

Element 4: full front view

Element 5: part-open bud

A composite design using elements shown on page 60. To emulate this design, see instructions overleaf.

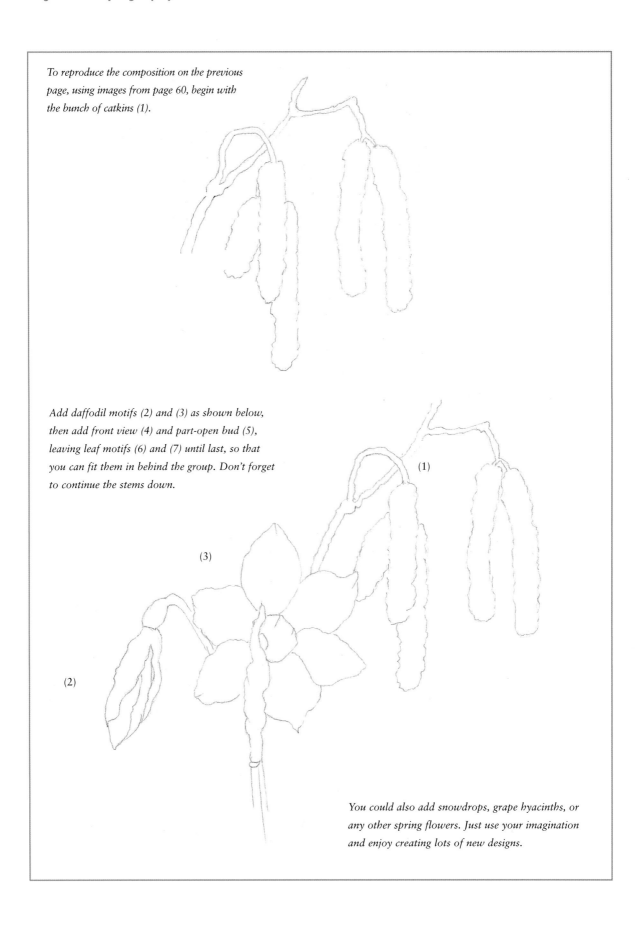

To reproduce the composition on the previous page, using images from page 60, begin with the bunch of catkins (1).

Add daffodil motifs (2) and (3) as shown below, then add front view (4) and part-open bud (5), leaving leaf motifs (6) and (7) until last, so that you can fit them in behind the group. Don't forget to continue the stems down.

(1)

(3)

(2)

You could also add snowdrops, grape hyacinths, or any other spring flowers. Just use your imagination and enjoy creating lots of new designs.

Tracing the designs

Materials and Equipment

Tracing paper (A4 minimum)
HB pencil
Ruler
Masking tape (low tack)
Pencil sharpener (or knife)
Black carbon paper, or tracing-down
    paper (instructions for making your
    own are given on page 8)

The materials and equipment required for tracing the designs

Method

1. Place the tracing paper over your chosen design. To make sure it doesn't slip, use small pieces of masking tape to hold it in place.   .

2. With a sharp, pointed pencil, carefully draw over the design outline, keeping to the outer edge of the lines. Put in any details you think you may need, such as eyes, leaf veins, brickwork, and so on.

3. Before removing the tracing paper, carefully remove one or two pieces of the masking tape and ease up the tracing paper to check that you haven't missed out any part of the design.

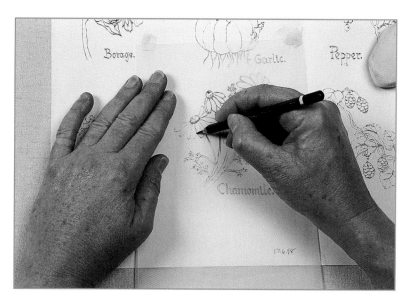

Drawing over the outline of the design

Making your own carbon paper

Home-made carbon paper is easy to make and better than the bought variety, because the lines can be erased more easily.

Materials and Equipment

Sheet of A4 layout paper (from art shops)
HB or B pencil
Soft tissues

Method

1. Carefully place the sheet of layout paper on a drawing board or similar surface. Take care, as layout paper is quite thin and could tear.

2. Cover the whole surface with pencil. Place the pencil strokes very close together, first in one direction then another, until the whole surface of the sheet has a good even covering of 'lead' (pencil dust). When you have finished, there should be no white paper showing.

3. Once you are sure that the paper is well coated with pencil, polish off the dust with soft tissues until no more lead comes off onto them. Your carbon paper is then ready to use.

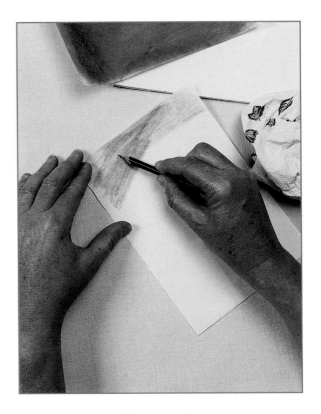

Covering every part of the paper with pencil to make home-made carbon paper

Enlarging and reducing the designs

The easiest way to enlarge or reduce a design is to use a photocopier, which can usually be found in office supplies shops and libraries. Most of these machines will enlarge and reduce in stages if you wish, by 50%, 25% and so on. You will have to pay a small fee but it is easier and quicker than drawing grids and painstakingly copying your design into the corresponding square. Alternatively, if you have access to a computer, scanner and printer, then you could use these to enlarge or reduce. You can buy specialist enlargers and reducers but they are expensive.

Whichever method you use, it is a good idea to keep the copies on file, so that you can use them again.

Transferring the designs

Materials and Equipment

Tracing of a design
Pencil
Carbon or tracing-down paper
Item on which you want to place the design

Method

1. If you are working on paper or card, make sure it is clean and free from grease. If you are working on wood, then make sure you have sanded it very smooth and removed any dust left on the surface after sanding.

2. Place your carbon paper (or tracing-down paper) on the surface you are going to work on, lead side down.

3. Position your traced design over it, and attach both pieces of paper to the surface with masking tape.

4. Draw carefully over the design outline using a sharp, pointed pencil. Before you do too much, check that the image is transferring onto the surface you are working on. If it isn't showing, you can try one of two things: either add more lead to the tracing down paper or press a little harder when going over the lines.

Types of wood for pyrography

Hardwoods – sycamore, birch, beech, lime and hornbeam – are the most suitable woods for pyrography. Sycamore and beech are the easiest to obtain from specialist suppliers of pyrography blanks and, being light coloured, they show off the work to its best advantage. They are also nicely grained and, with a little imagination, you can use the pattern of the grain to enhance your designs.

Good quality birch plywood is an acceptable substitute for the more expensive hardwoods, and can be obtained from local wood merchants. It has a creamy-beige, smooth finish, with a nice grain, and takes pyrography well. Ask your suppliers if they have offcuts at a cheaper price. Do not purchase ordinary builders' plywood, as this is of poorer quality, reddish in colour, and has a coarse grain.

Veneer is also suitable for pyrography, provided it is firmly attached to something more solid, such as MDF (medium-density fibre board). Again, the lighter-coloured veneers are better to work on than the darker ones. MDF is very cheap and available from your local DIY store, but shop around as prices can vary. Generally, the lighter, smoother-grained woods produce a better and finer finish than the darker, coarser-grained ones such as oak and mahogany.

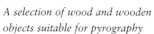

A selection of wood and wooden objects suitable for pyrography

A word of warning about working with MDF and woods. The Health and Safety Executive recommend that the dust from all hardwoods, English or tropical, be treated with the utmost caution and a protective mask should be worn when sanding these or carrying out any process which produces dust. MDF is not harmful in its solid state.

Adding Colour

The use of colour can add greatly to the appeal of your designs, but you will need to select the right kind of paints for the item you are painting on, which will depend on how and where it is going to be used.

Wood can be painted with watercolours and then sealed with clear varnish. This treatment would be suitable for any item being kept inside. However, if the work is to be used outside, it would be wise to use acrylic paints, as these are more hard-wearing and resistant to fading in strong sunlight. I recommend using watercolours for work on paper and card. Of course, you do not have to use paint and you may prefer to use coloured inks, coloured pencils or pen and ink. The choice is yours, but do remember that whatever you choose, it should enhance your work.

Whatever paints you decide to use, it is helpful to know a little about them, and how to mix them, so that you can make a wider range of colours from the limited palette.

Suggested Materials and Equipment

Paints, appropriate for the item being decorated
Paintbrushes, in assorted sizes:
  Acrylic brushes for acrylic paints
  Watercolour brushes for watercolours
Water container
Old saucer or plate to mix on
Special stay-wet paper palette for acrylics

The paints and equipment required for colouring pyrography

Mixing colours

A wide range of colours can be mixed from the
following basic colours:

Alizarin crimson
Ultramarine blue
Vermilion hue
Raw umber
Cadmium yellow pale
Payne's grey
Chinese white

Inner circle
Primary colours

Outer circle
Secondary colours

*A simple colour wheel, showing primary and
secondary colours*

Basic Palette

Alizarin crimson

Ultramarine blue

Vermilion hue

Raw umber

Cadmium yellow pale

Payne's grey

Chinese white

Mixes

Raw umber and ultramarine

Raw umber, ultramarine and a little cadmium yellow pale

Raw umber and cadmium yellow pale

Payne's grey and cadmium yellow pale

Payne's grey and alizarin crimson

Payne's grey and alizarin crimson, but with more Payne's grey

The basic palette and a selection of colour mixes

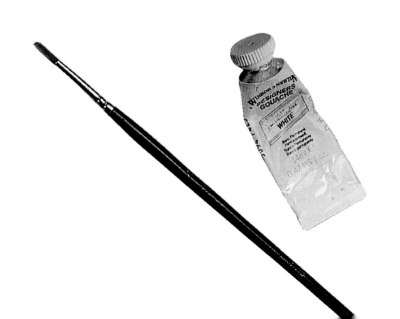

Method for mixing colours

You can increase your range of colours by mixing together combinations of your basic palette. To do this, you must carefully control the amount of one colour as you add it to another. Below I give an example using ultramarine blue and cadmium yellow pale.

1. Make a pool of yellow. Do not make it too thin, and make enough to allow you to mix up quite a few different shades of green. Take a little of this paint from the pool and paint a square of yellow.

2. Do not clean the brush, but pick up a very small amount of blue and mix this into the whole pool of yellow. When fully mixed in, paint a second square next to the yellow one, leaving a little space between the two.

3. Repeat step 2 again and again, gradually adding small amounts of blue to the pool of yellow. The yellow should gradually turn green. After each addition of blue, paint a sample square of the new mix.

Applying colour

Do not add colour until you are absolutely sure that you have completed the drawing. Then, mix up the paint you require and add water to dilute it into a fairly thin, transparent colour.

Using a no. 2 or no. 4 brush, paint in the chosen area. If the colour looks washed out, add more pigment to the colour you mixed previously and paint over it. It is better to start with the paint too thin, as a thicker paint makes the finished work look lifeless and solid.

Whichever medium you choose to colour your work, remember that it should be used to enhance and complement it, rather than overpower or obscure it.

It is a good idea to experiment with mixing basic colours together and to keep a record of which colour you added to which. You can note these mixes in a series of sample squares as shown below.

Chapter

2

The Designs

Puppy in basket

Dog with a frisbee

Puppy's head

Cat sunbathing on paving stones

Three studies of cats

Kitten

Tabby cat up a tree

Racehorse

Riding pony

Horse and rider

Donkey

Heavy horse

Pony

Heavy horse

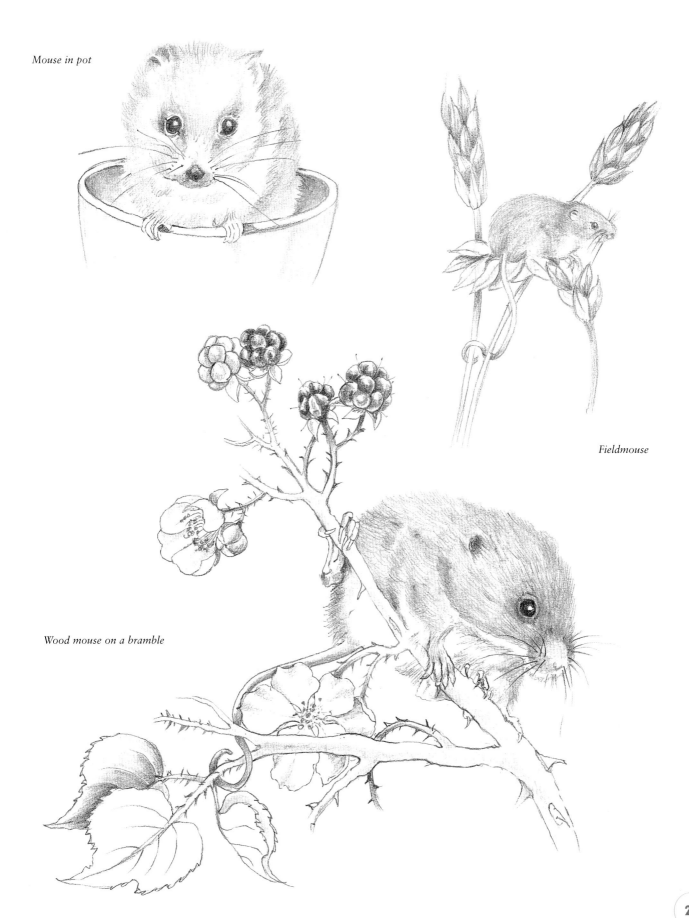

Mouse in pot

Fieldmouse

Wood mouse on a bramble

Rabbit motifs

*Wren on a pot
of pansies*

Bluetit

Bluetit on a hazel twig

Kingfisher

Robin on a pot with woodbine growing around it

Macaw

Swan with cygnet

Pink flamingo

*Boats and
harbour scenes*

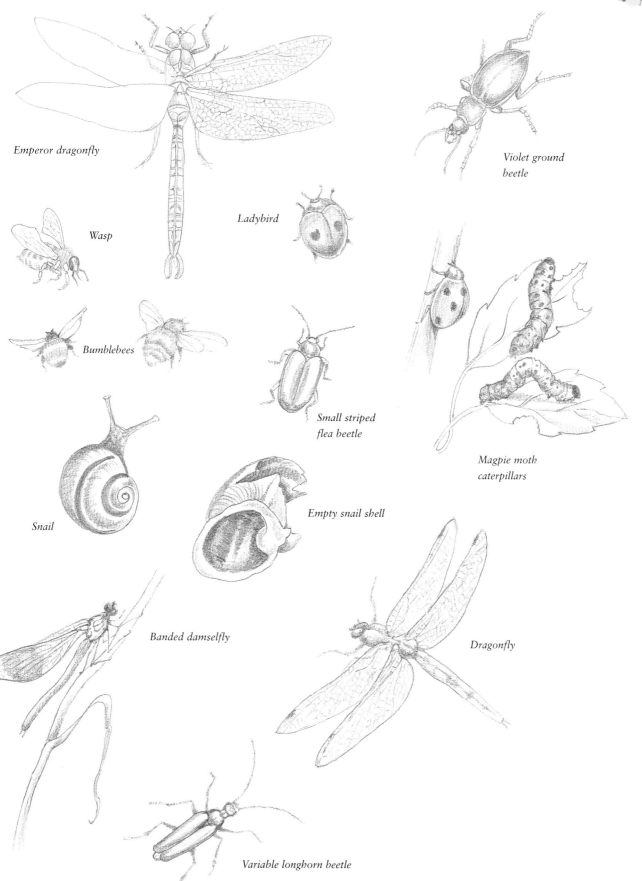

Emperor dragonfly

Violet ground
beetle

Wasp

Ladybird

Bumblebees

Small striped
flea beetle

Magpie moth
caterpillars

Snail

Empty snail shell

Banded damselfly

Dragonfly

Variable longhorn beetle

Large white

Large white with
wings closed

Orange Tip with
wings closed

Peacock butterfly

Marbled White

Common Blue with
wings open and
wings closed

Small Tortoiseshell
butterfly

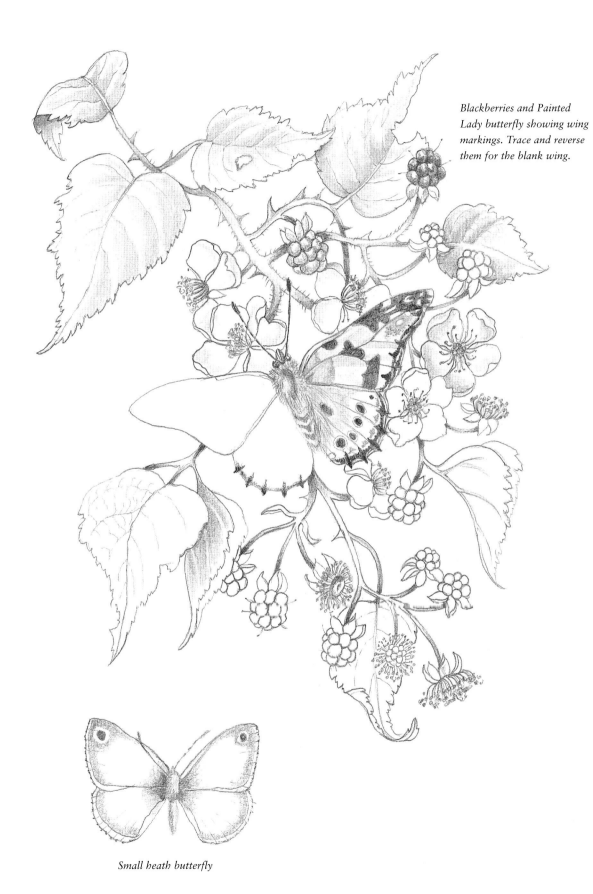

Blackberries and Painted Lady butterfly showing wing markings. Trace and reverse them for the blank wing.

Small heath butterfly

Pigs feeding

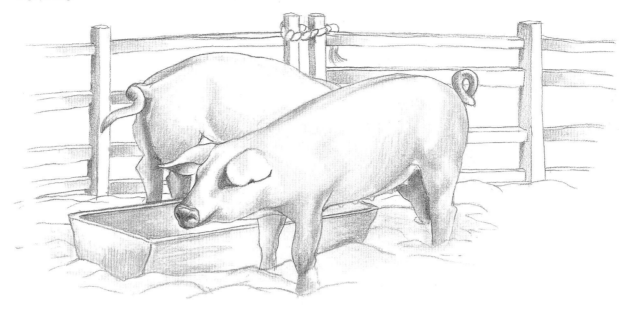

Cows at rest

Cows in pasture

Horse and cart

*Returning home
with the horses*

Ploughing

Sheepdog

Farmhands collecting the sheaves

Haystack

Milk churns on a handcart

Old tractor

Windmill

Farm with outbuildings

Thatched cottage

Stone almshouses

Two old cottages

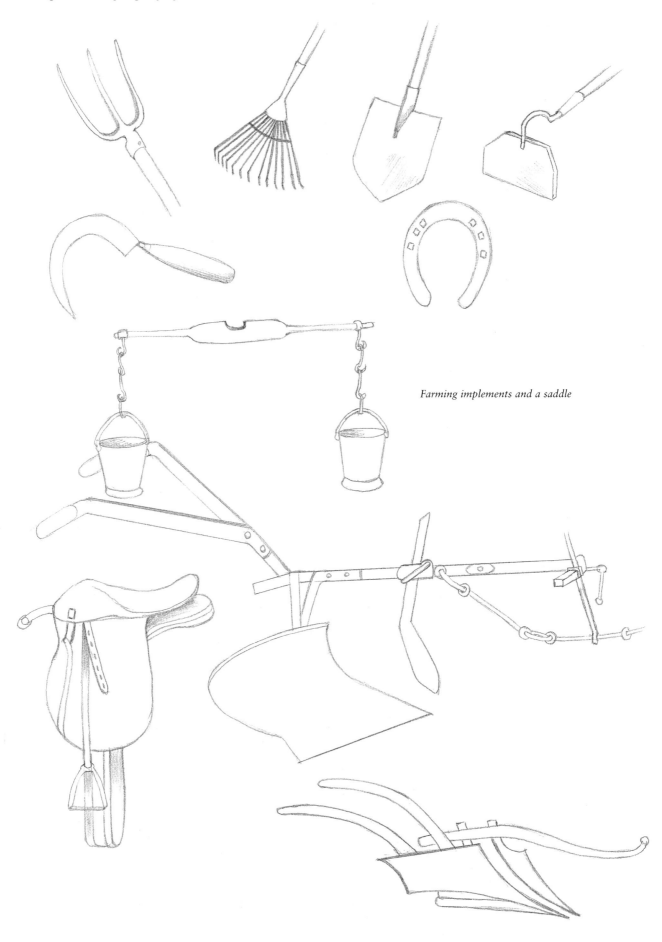

Farming implements and a saddle

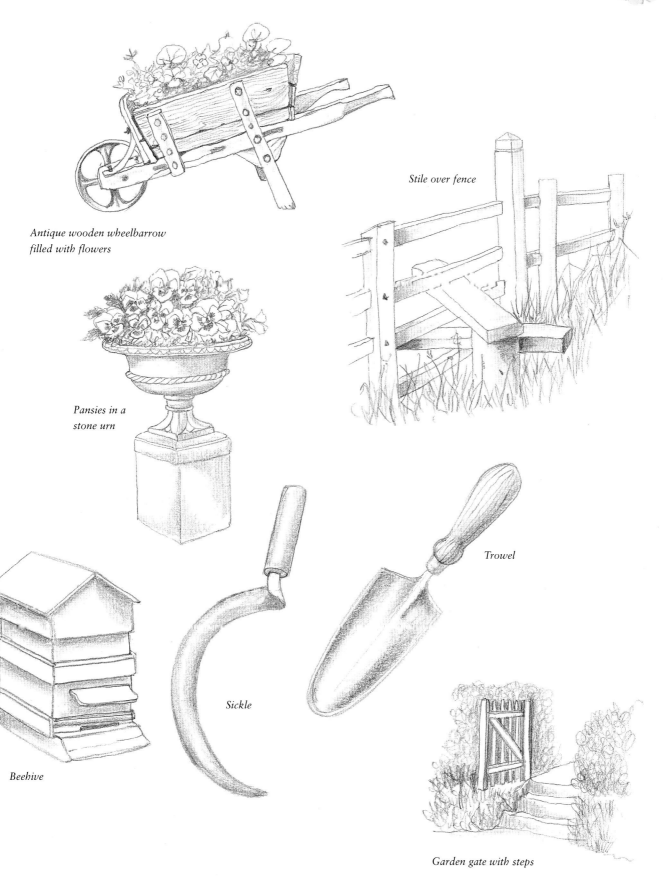

Antique wooden wheelbarrow
filled with flowers

Stile over fence

Pansies in a
stone urn

Trowel

Beehive

Sickle

Garden gate with steps

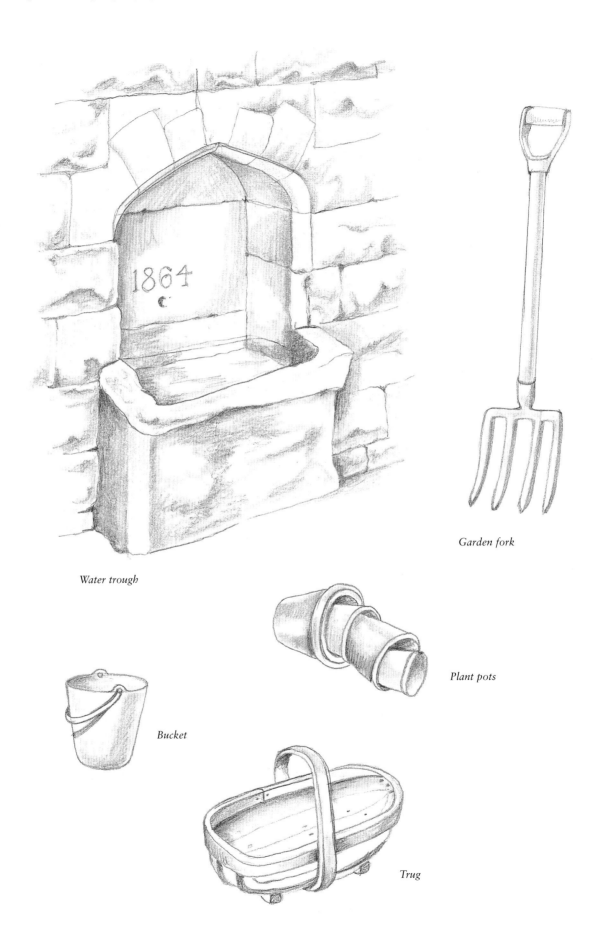

Water trough

Garden fork

Plant pots

Bucket

Trug

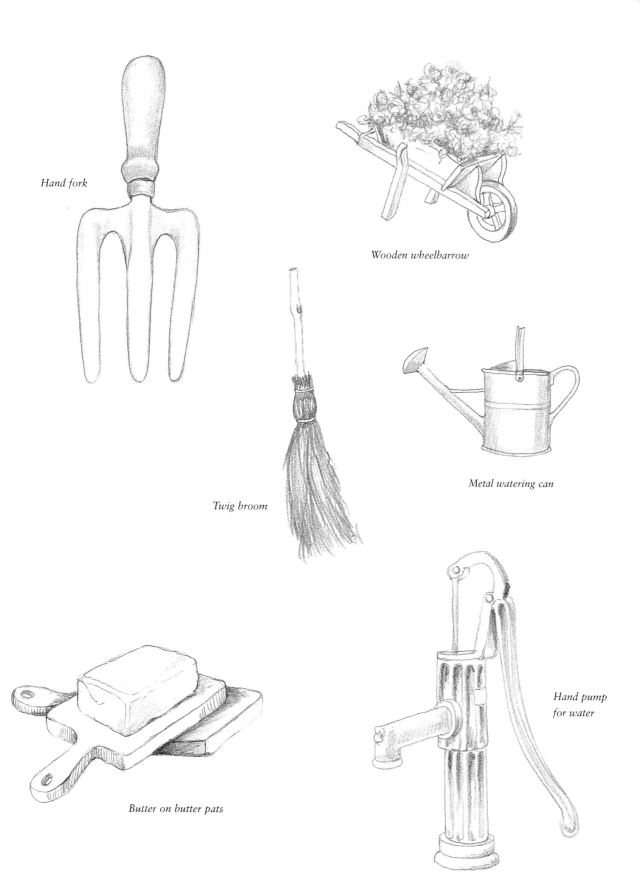

Hand fork

Wooden wheelbarrow

Twig broom

Metal watering can

Hand pump
for water

Butter on butter pats

Wrought-iron gate with garden view

Sheaves of corn

Haystacks

Open field gate

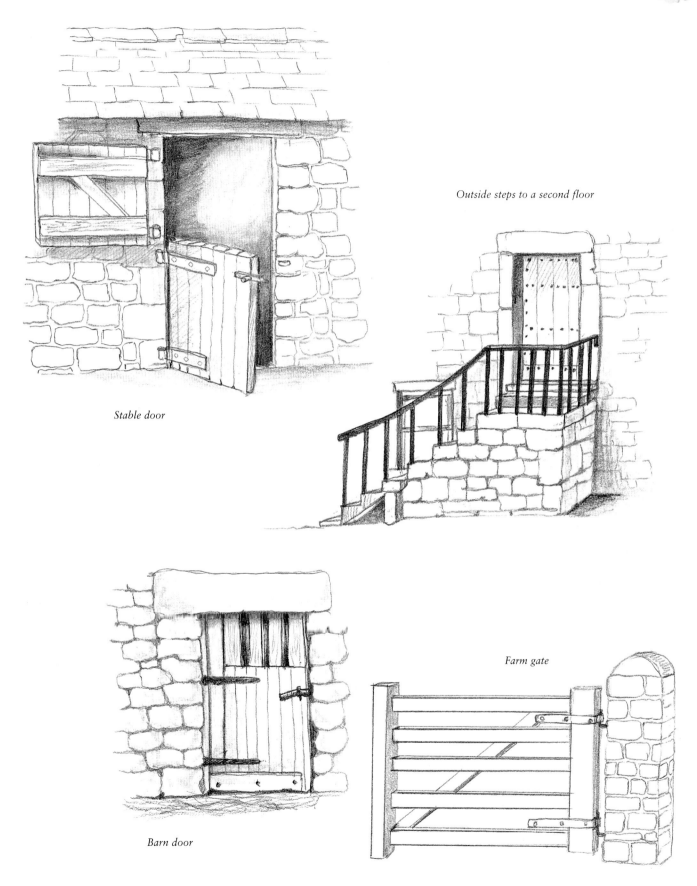

Stable door

Outside steps to a second floor

Barn door

Farm gate

French anemone

Broom

Convolvulus

Daffodil

Edelweiss

Fritillary

Grape hyacinth

Honeysuckle

Bearded iris

Japonica

Kaffir lily

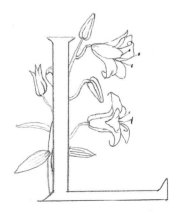

Lily

Magnolia

Nicotiana (tobacco plant)

Osteospurmum

Pansy

Quercus (oak)

Rose

Snowdrop

Tulip

Ulmus (elm)

Violet

Wisteria

Xeranthemum annum

Yucca

Zinnia

Painted examples of flower and animal alphabets.
The letters would look very effective in gold, too.

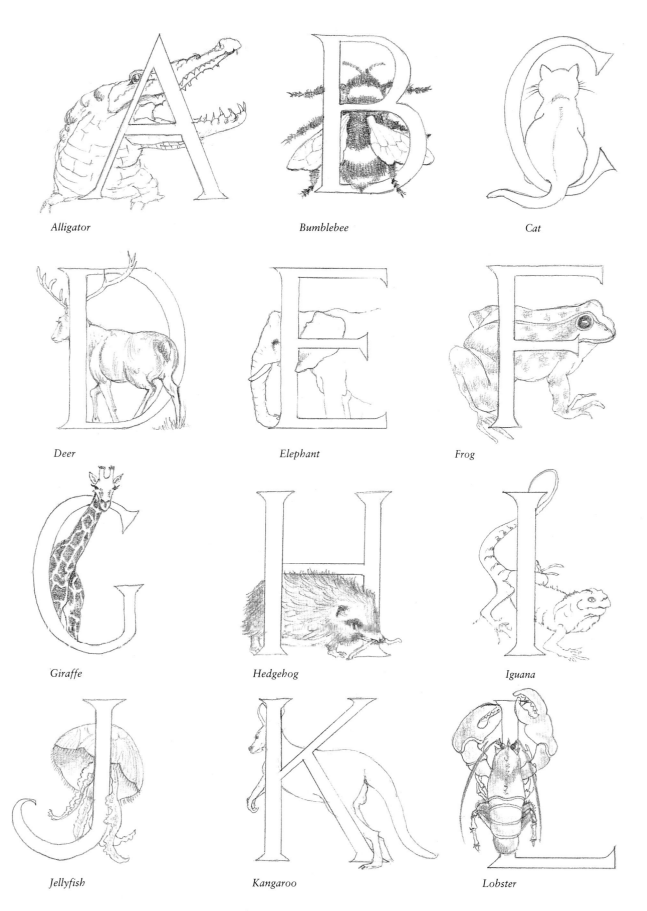

Alligator

Bumblebee

Cat

Deer

Elephant

Frog

Giraffe

Hedgehog

Iguana

Jellyfish

Kangaroo

Lobster

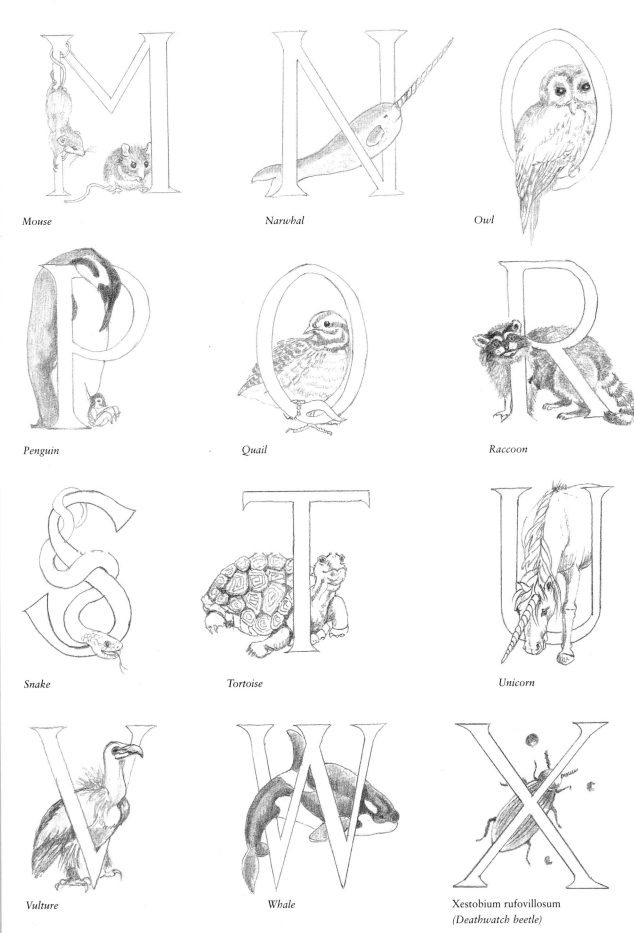

Mouse

Narwhal

Owl

Penguin

Quail

Raccoon

Snake

Tortoise

Unicorn

Vulture

Whale

Xestobium rufovillosum
(Deathwatch beetle)

Yak

Zebra

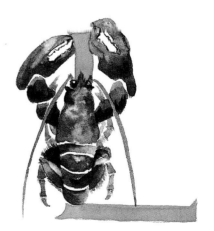

To achieve the mottled effect on this letter 'D', I ran the two paint colours together while they were still wet.

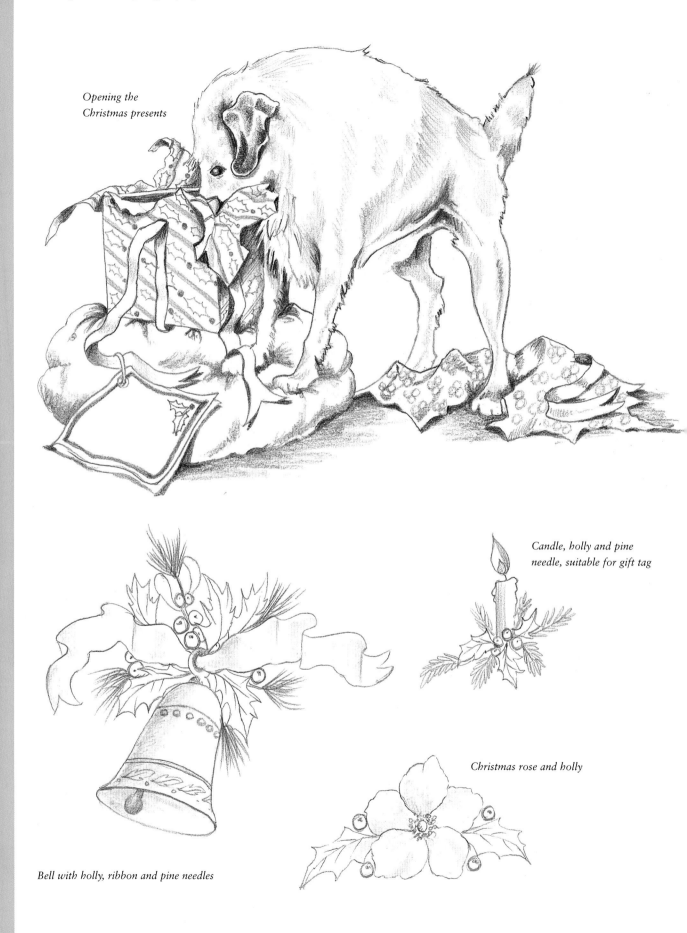

*Opening the
Christmas presents*

*Candle, holly and pine
needle, suitable for gift tag*

Christmas rose and holly

Bell with holly, ribbon and pine needles

*Christmas wreath with poinsettia,
Christmas roses, holly and mistletoe*

*Pine cone with holly and
ribbon, suitable for gift tags*

Mistletoe and ribbon

Christmas tree bauble

*Christmas baubles, candle,
ivy and pine cones*

Christmas pudding on
platter, with holly

Christmas stocking
with holly, pine
cones and needles

Ribbon frame for
a snow scene of a
village church

Christmas lantern with holly

A selection of Christmas borders which can be used to edge cards with a central Christmas design

Father Christmas with a
sack and Christmas tree

Snowman

Traditional carol
singers

'Christmas Star' bauble

Easter egg

Primroses and forget-me-nots, with briar stems

Easter bunny

Narcissi with 'crown-of-thorns'

Easter rabbit in a basket

Easter bonnet

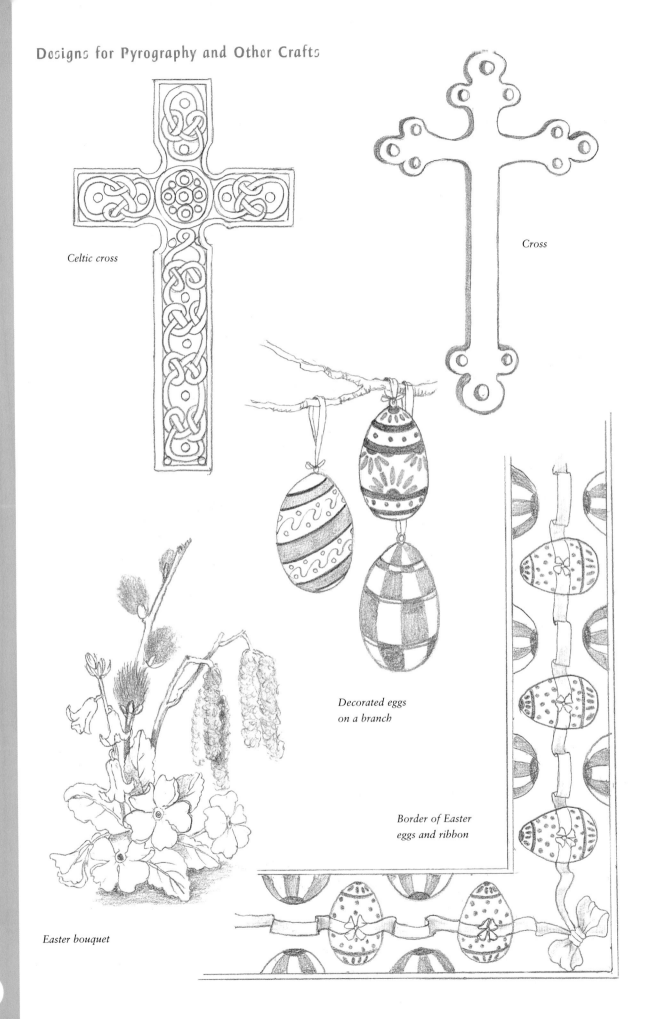

Celtic cross

Cross

Decorated eggs
on a branch

Border of Easter
eggs and ribbon

Easter bouquet

Entwined wedding rings

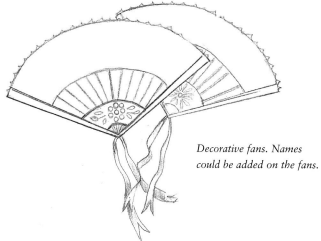

Decorative fans. Names could be added on the fans.

A motif for any celebration or anniversary

Wedding horseshoe

The corner blanks on this design could contain initials and/or numbers

Wedding anniversary bells. Add numbers to match the anniversary.

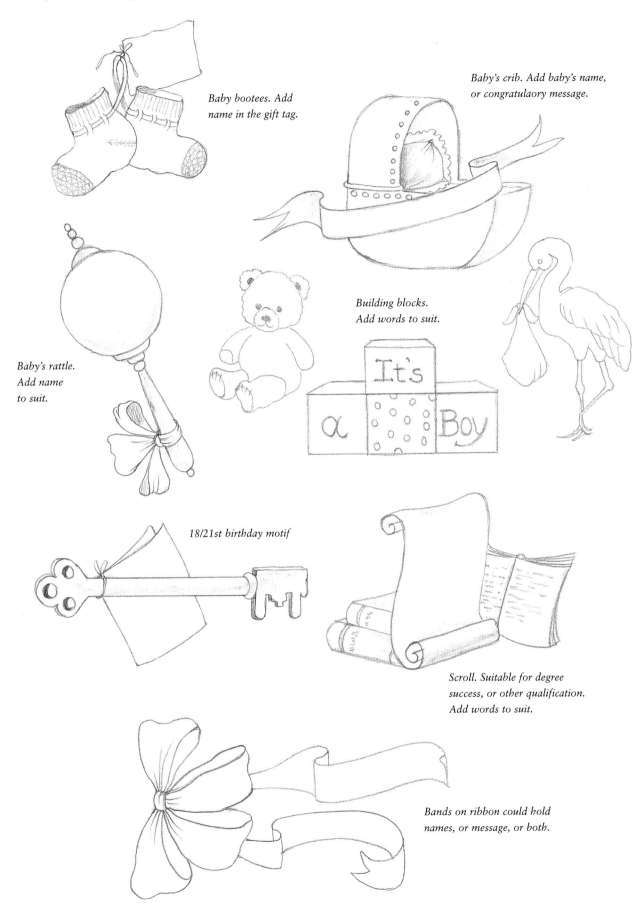

Baby bootees. Add name in the gift tag.

Baby's crib. Add baby's name, or congratulaory message.

Baby's rattle. Add name to suit.

Building blocks. Add words to suit.

It's a Boy

18/21st birthday motif

Scroll. Suitable for degree success, or other qualification. Add words to suit.

Bands on ribbon could hold names, or message, or both.

Heart with ribbon
edge and bouquet
of red roses

Design with hearts.
Suitable for valentine
card or gift tag.

Names could be added
on the band or the hearts.

This border could be used with any of the smaller motifs.

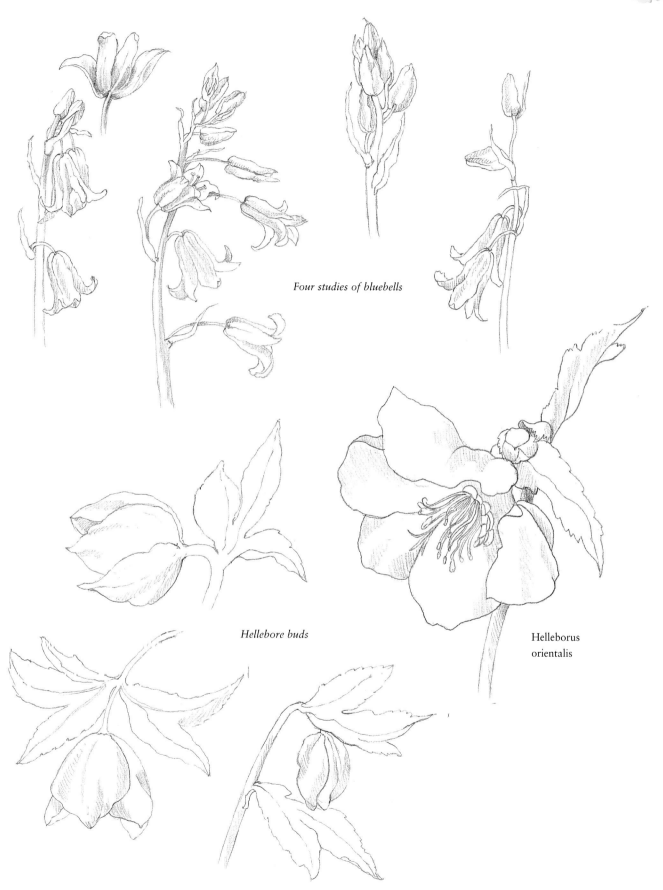

Four studies of bluebells

Hellebore buds

Helleborus
orientalis

Studies of dwarf daffodils
and their leaves

Snake's-head
fritillary

Grape hyacinths

Catkins

Watercolour pansies. Further examples are shown overleaf.

Posy of pansies, buds, leaves and ribbon. For ideas on colour and 'faces' of pansies, see the painted examples on pages 61–2.

Posy of violets

Snowdrops with ribbon loops

Bouquet of roses

Studies of pansy flowers, buds and leaves, snowdrops, violets and roses. These elements can be added to suitable designs in the book, or you can use them to create a new one.

A study of pansies. See the paintings of pansy faces on pp. 61–2 for ideas of colours to use. You could also add a bee in the left-hand corner, or a bee or a ladybird on a leaf (see images on page 27).

A pansy heart

Rose, with water droplet

Bearded Iris

Wisteria

Garden pinks: this variety is called 'Doris'. You could use the design, without the dark bands on some petals, and copy the paintings of pinks shown on page 81.

Crown imperial fritillary (orange)

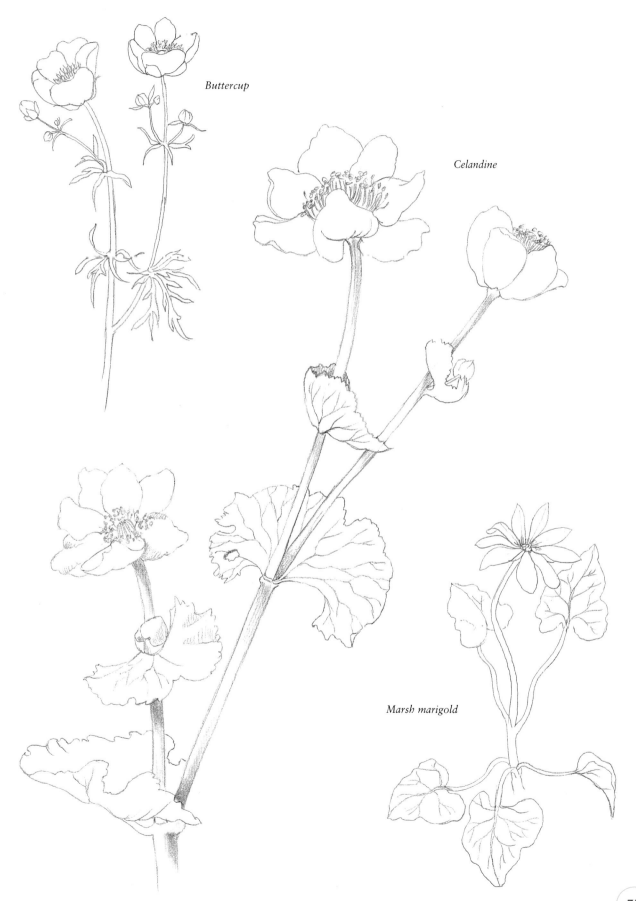

Buttercup

Celandine

Marsh marigold

Water lily in flower

Water lily buds

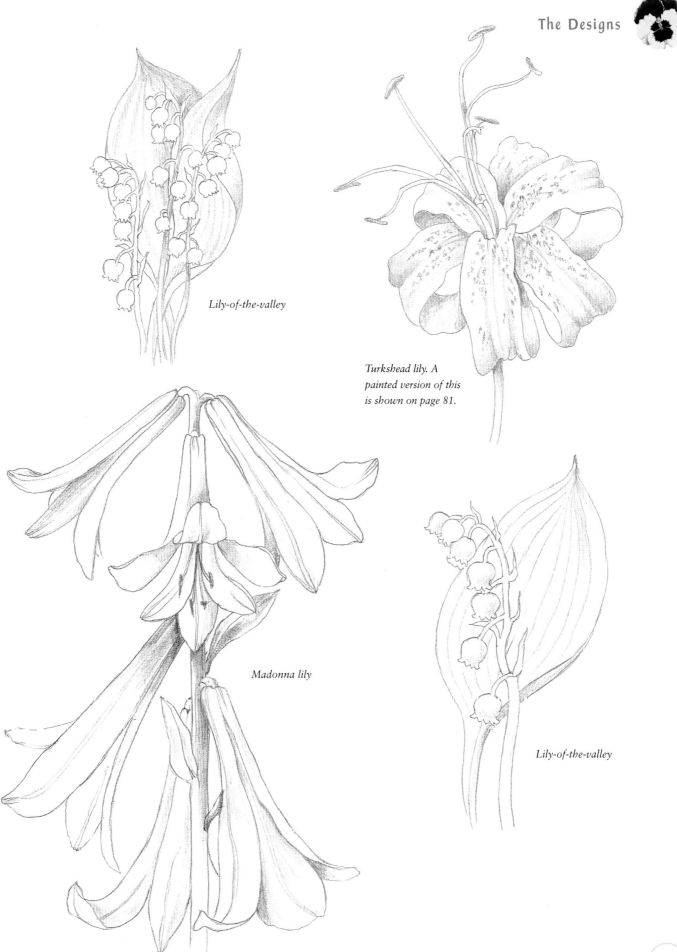

Lily-of-the-valley

Turkshead lily. A
painted version of this
is shown on page 81.

Madonna lily

Lily-of-the-valley

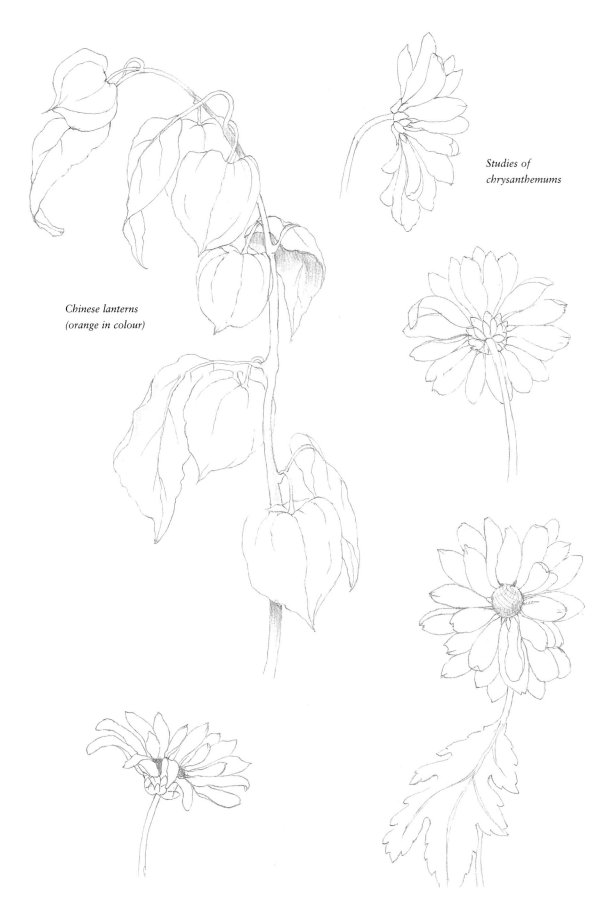

Studies of
chrysanthemums

Chinese lanterns
(orange in colour)

Dahlia studies

Freesia

Freesia bud

Honeysuckle

Hanging begonia

Turkshead lily. This shows
how the design on page
77 could look, if painted.

Garden pink ('Doris')

Garden pink
('Raspberry ripple')

Studies of Anemone blanda, *an early
spring-flowering bulb, which can be a
vivid pale blue/lilac, white or pink.*

Aconites: a vivid yellow in colour

Narcissus and polyanthus flowers, suitable for a corner or central position.

Oval design using ribbon, narcissus, polyanthus and tiny blue forget-me-nots.

Corner design using a polyanthus flower and ribbon

This design could be used with the corner design above to frame a rectangle.

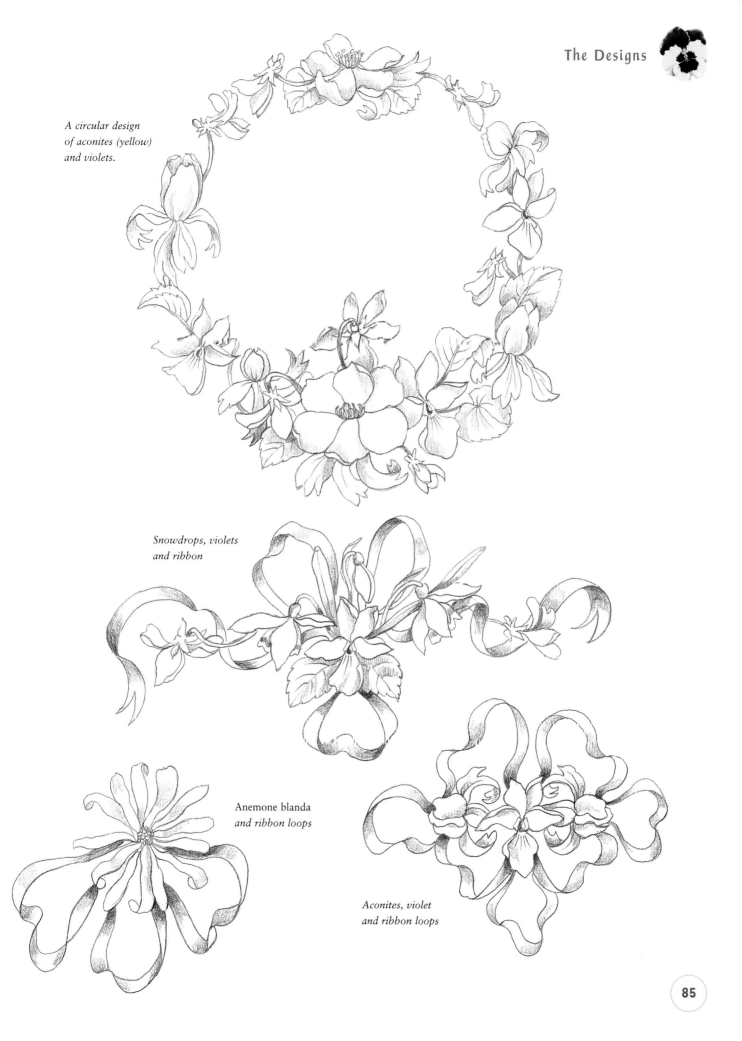

A circular design
of aconites (yellow)
and violets.

Snowdrops, violets
and ribbon

Anemone blanda
and ribbon loops

Aconites, violet
and ribbon loops

A swag of drapes, a violet centrepiece, and corners

Pansy and ribbon wreath

Snowdrops and ivy corner motif

Aconite and bar motif

Narcissus and ribbon

Main design featuring narcissus,
primulas, ivy and forget-me-nots

Corner motif using ivy
with a primula

Spray of polyanthus
and narcissus

*Rose, daisy and honeysuckle,
with bumblebee*

These borders would work
particularly well with the
designs on pages 62, 63, 65
and 66.

The small motifs could
be used for gift tags, bookmarks, etc, and the border
lines could be painted with
gold paint.

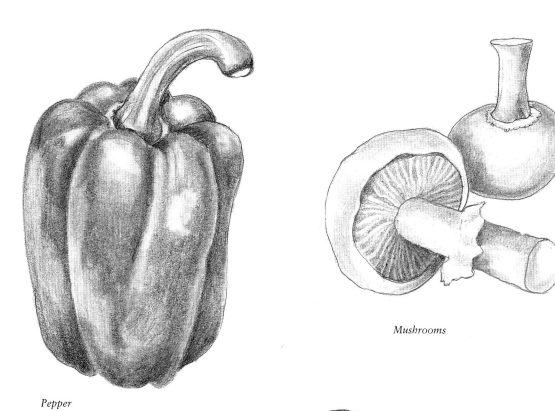

Pepper

Mushrooms

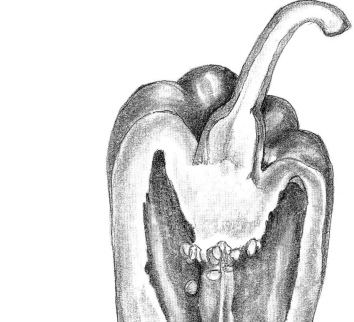

Pepper cut in half

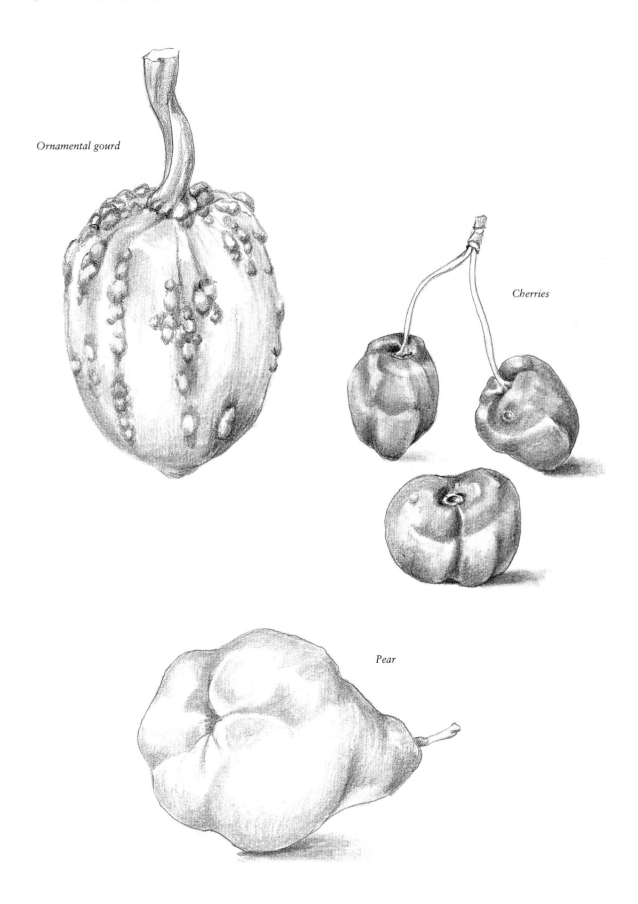

Ornamental gourd

Cherries

Pear

Bunch of grapes

Cape gooseberries

Strawberries

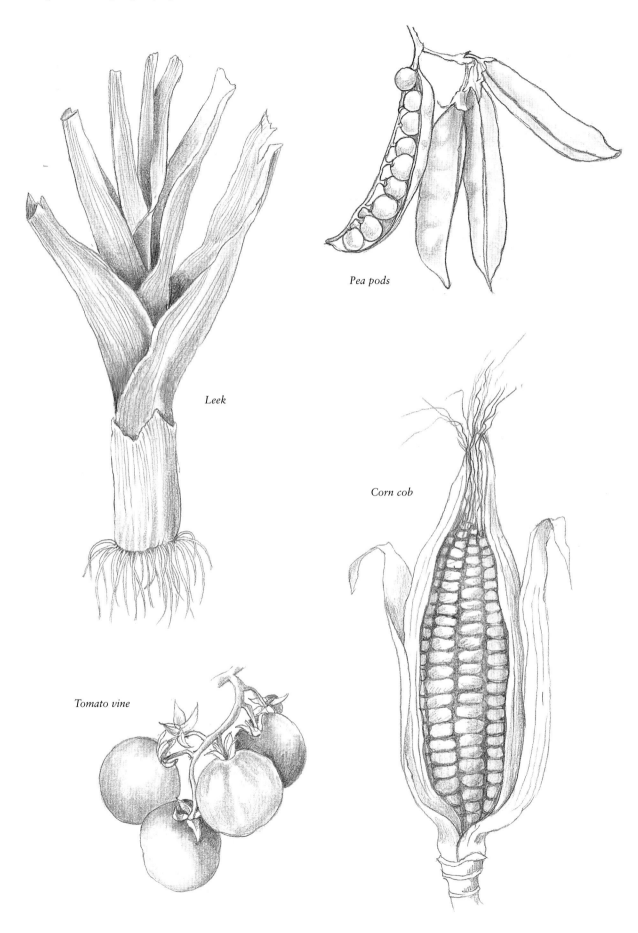

Pea pods

Leek

Corn cob

Tomato vine

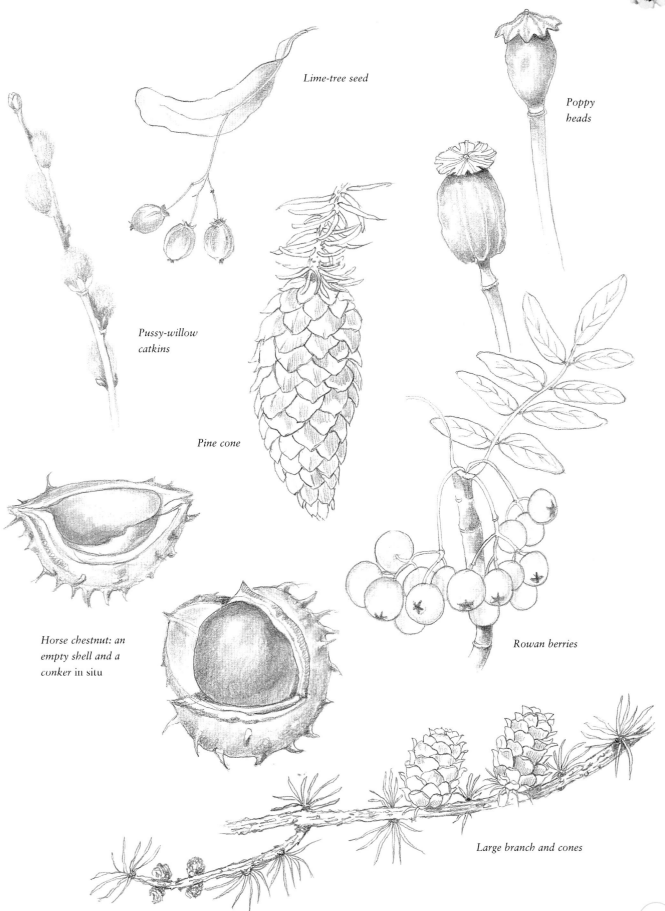

Lime-tree seed

Poppy heads

Pussy-willow catkins

Pine cone

Horse chestnut: an empty shell and a conker in situ

Rowan berries

Large branch and cones

Scots pine

Elm

Spruce

Pollarded willows

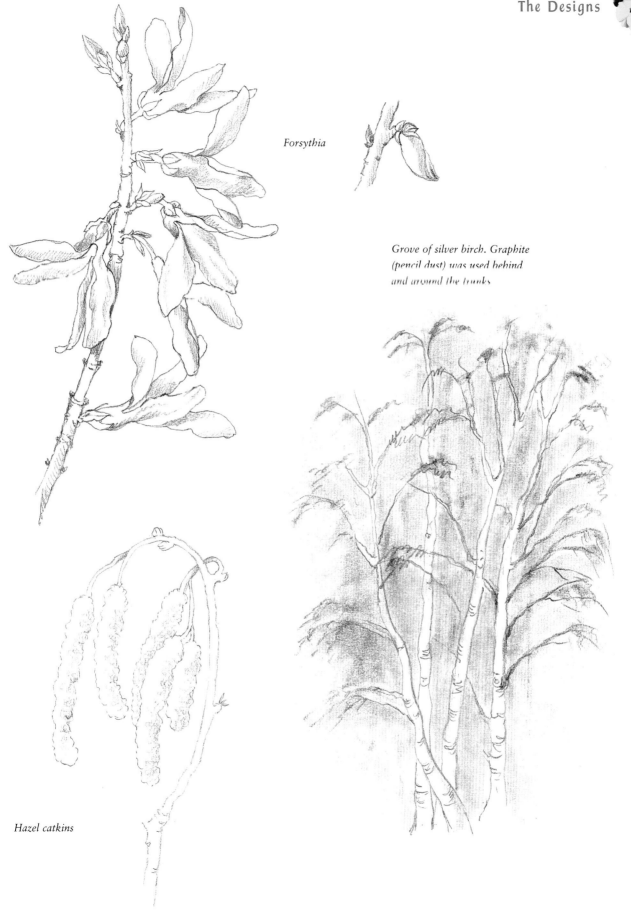

Forsythia

Grove of silver birch. Graphite (pencil dust) was used behind and around the trunks

Hazel catkins

A selection of motifs. These could be enlarged to go on cards, or used to decorate other items for presents.

Assorted ribbon bows

Chapter

3

Other Sources
for Designs

Other sources for designs

You can make additions to the designs in this book by collecting your own material as a source of inspiration. Magazines, photographs, reference books and films could all trigger your creative urge, as well as found items such as shells, plants and flowers. Visits to museums, art galleries, wildlife parks, zoos, and the countryside will also provide you with a great variety of visual stimulation. Record the images on film, in a sketchbook, or on a camcorder, and file the information in some kind of order, if possible, so that you can access it easily.

NOTE
Before you use any material not personally filmed or sketched by you, check that you are not infringing anyone's copyright, as it is an offence to do so.

Right: *A collection of found objects, photos and sketches that are useful sources of inspiration*

66 The Japanese
water iris is a lovely
t to have in
den 99

An iris well worth considering
with the unfortunate name of Iri
pseudacorus var. *bastardii*. It is a free-
flowering deciduous variety that
of room as it can grow up to 1.8m   for a considerable period from
(72in) in ideal conditions.   summer onwards. It is some
listed as 'Sulphur Queen' a
is incorrect.
'Variegata' (AGM) is a su
which has yellow- and gre
foliage early in the season
fades to green. It flowers i
summer.

From Japan,
Iris ensata 'Aioi'

66 Iris laevigata can
be grown from seed –
an ideal way to raise
new plants – b
some

Chapter

4

The Gallery

Pyrography

DECORATIVE PLAQUE
This uses the 'Thatched cottage' design on page 35.

DECORATIVE BOX
This was a sweet box holding Turkish delight. The wood it is made from is very soft to pyrograph, so the design is not as 'fine' in line as it would be on a hardwood such as sycamore. The water lilies, which are the design on page 76, are tinted with watercolour.

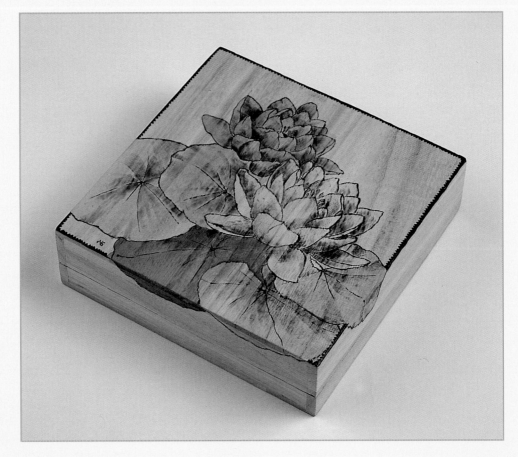

RIMMED WOODEN PLATE
This uses the mouse design from page 21. One of the blackberries has been used as a border design around the rim.

LARGE PLATE
This combines two designs from page 31: the farmhouse from 'Horse and cart', and 'Returning home with the horses'.

China

TEAPOT
This uses the pansy design from page 89, painted in acrylics.

THIMBLE
Here I have used the violet bud design from page 67. I used acrylic paints, because that was what I had to hand. If you use ceramic paints instead, choose those that do not require traditional firing in a kiln.

TABLE-NAPKIN HOLDERS
For these, both the pansy and the violet designs from pages 67 and 89 have been slightly adapted to fit the available space. Acrylic paint was used.

Cards

Most of the designs are suitable for cards, and they do not
have to be painted. Instead, you could cut them out in
coloured papers or fabrics, or make them in parchment
craft. The chance to use your imagination is without limit.

VALENTINE CARD
*The design from page
58 was first traced onto
the card, then the hearts
were traced onto a foil
paper, cut out and stuck
over the design. Space
has been left underneath
the design for your
chosen message.*

BABY'S RATTLE DESIGN
*The rattle used here is
the design from page
56, in watercolour.
Appropriate wording
could be added, such as
'It's a boy!'.*

DECOUPAGE CARD
*The violet design, from
page 67 was traced three
times onto thin paper,
painted and then cut out.
The first painted one was
stuck down flat. For the
second flower, I used
only the side petals and
front one, slightly curling
them. The third flower I
used in the same way as
the second.*

CHRISTMAS CARD
*This Christmas stocking
design, from page 50,
has been painted in
watercolours.*

ASSORTED GIFT TAGS
*The gift tags shown here, and overleaf, demonstrate how the
designs can be used to great effect on coloured paper and card.*

MORE GIFT TAGS

BOOKMARKS
Designs have been repeated down the length of these bookmarks. Again, coloured papers have been used effectively.

112

DECORATIVE BOX
Brown cardboard box painted with two coats of emulsion paint. Fieldmouse design from page 21, painted in gouache paint.

PHOTO FRAME
Brown cardboard base covered with two coats of emulsion paint and allowed to dry. Again, the design, which features 'Narcissus and ribbon' from page 87, and a ribbon bow from page 99, has been painted in gouache.

MINIATURES

The designs can also be used to produce framed miniatures. Here I have framed painted versions of 'Dog with a frisbee', from page 16, and 'Kingfisher' from page 23.

About the Author

Norma Gregory trained to be a teacher and worked initially in comprehensive schools. She then moved into adult education, obtaining a postgraduate degree in adult education from Leeds University in Yorkshire, England. In time, she became a Director of Adult and Community Education. In 1992 she took early retirement and resumed her interests in art and crafts after a 30-year gap.

In recent years, Norma has been made an associate of The British Watercolour Society and a member of The Society of Floral Painters. She is also a member of a botanical illustration society and is channelling her interests and energies into this particular field of painting. She runs flower-painting courses at adult residential colleges, and once a month she runs an art workshop in her village in East Anglia, England.

Index

TITLES AVAILABLE FROM
GMC Publications
BOOKS

WOODCARVING

Beginning Woodcarving	*GMC Publications*
Carving Architectural Detail in Wood: The Classical Tradition	
	Frederick Wilbur
Carving Birds & Beasts	*GMC Publications*
Carving Classical Styles in Wood	*Frederick Wilbur*
Carving the Human Figure: Studies in Wood and Stone	*Dick Onians*
Carving Nature: Wildlife Studies in Wood	*Frank Fox-Wilson*
Celtic Carved Lovespoons: 30 Patterns	*Sharon Littley & Clive Griffin*
Decorative Woodcarving (New Edition)	*Jeremy Williams*
Elements of Woodcarving	*Chris Pye*
Figure Carving in Wood: Human and Animal Forms	*Sara Wilkinson*
Lettercarving in Wood: A Practical Course	*Chris Pye*
Relief Carving in Wood: A Practical Introduction	*Chris Pye*
Woodcarving for Beginners	*GMC Publications*
Woodcarving Made Easy	*Cynthia Rogers*
Woodcarving Tools, Materials & Equipment (New Edition in 2 vols.)	
	Chris Pye

WOODTURNING

Bowl Turning Techniques Masterclass	*Tony Boase*
Chris Child's Projects for Woodturners	*Chris Child*
Decorating Turned Wood: The Maker's Eye	
	Liz & Michael O'Donnell
Green Woodwork	*Mike Abbott*
A Guide to Work-Holding on the Lathe	*Fred Holder*
Keith Rowley's Woodturning Projects	*Keith Rowley*
Making Screw Threads in Wood	*Fred Holder*
Segmented Turning: A Complete Guide	*Ron Hampton*
Turned Boxes: 50 Designs	*Chris Stott*
Turning Green Wood	*Michael O'Donnell*
Turning Pens and Pencils	*Kip Christensen & Rex Burningham*
Wood for Woodturners	*Mark Baker*
Woodturning: Forms and Materials	*John Hunnex*
Woodturning: A Foundation Course (New Edition)	*Keith Rowley*
Woodturning: A Fresh Approach	*Robert Chapman*
Woodturning: An Individual Approach	*Dave Regester*
Woodturning: A Source Book of Shapes	*John Hunnex*
Woodturning Masterclass	*Tony Boase*
Woodturning Projects: A Workshop Guide to Shapes	*Mark Baker*

WOODWORKING

Beginning Picture Marquetry	*Lawrence Threadgold*
Carcass Furniture	*GMC Publications*
Celtic Carved Lovespoons: 30 Patterns	*Sharon Littley & Clive Griffin*
Celtic Woodcraft	*Glenda Bennett*
Celtic Woodworking Projects	*Glenda Bennett*
Complete Woodfinishing (Revised Edition)	*Ian Hosker*
David Charlesworth's Furniture-Making Techniques	
	David Charlesworth
David Charlesworth's Furniture-Making Techniques –	
Volume 2	*David Charlesworth*

Furniture Projects with the Router	*Kevin Ley*
Furniture Restoration (Practical Crafts)	*Kevin Jan Bonner*
Furniture Restoration: A Professional at Work	*John Lloyd*
Furniture Workshop	*Kevin Ley*
Green Woodwork	*Mike Abbott*
History of Furniture: Ancient to 1900	*Michael Huntley*
Intarsia: 30 Patterns for the Scrollsaw	*John Everett*
Making Heirloom Boxes	*Peter Lloyd*
Making Screw Threads in Wood	*Fred Holder*
Making Woodwork Aids and Devices	*Robert Wearing*
Mastering the Router	*Ron Fox*
Pine Furniture Projects for the Home	*Dave Mackenzie*
Router Magic: Jigs, Fixtures and Tricks to	
Unleash your Router's Full Potential	*Bill Hylton*
Router Projects for the Home	*GMC Publications*
Router Tips & Techniques	*Robert Wearing*
Routing: A Workshop Handbook	*Anthony Bailey*
Routing for Beginners (Revised and Expanded Edition)	
	Anthony Bailey
Stickmaking: A Complete Course	*Andrew Jones & Clive George*
Stickmaking Handbook	*Andrew Jones & Clive George*
Storage Projects for the Router	*GMC Publications*
Veneering: A Complete Course	*Ian Hosker*
Veneering Handbook	*Ian Hosker*
Wood: Identification & Use	*Terry Porter*
Woodworking Techniques and Projects	*Anthony Bailey*
Woodworking with the Router: Professional Router Techniques	
any Woodworker can Use	*Bill Hylton & Fred Matlack*

UPHOLSTERY

Upholstery: A Beginners' Guide	*David James*
Upholstery: A Complete Course (Revised Edition)	*David James*
Upholstery Restoration	*David James*
Upholstery Techniques & Projects	*David James*
Upholstery Tips and Hints	*David James*

DOLLS' HOUSES AND MINIATURES

1/12 Scale Character Figures for the Dolls' House	*James Carrington*
Americana in 1/12 Scale: 50 Authentic Projects	
	Joanne Ogreenc & Mary Lou Santovec
The Authentic Georgian Dolls' House	*Brian Long*
A Beginners' Guide to the Dolls' House Hobby	*Jean Nisbett*
Celtic, Medieval and Tudor Wall	
Hangings in 1/12 Scale Needlepoint	*Sandra Whitehead*
Creating Decorative Fabrics: Projects in 1/12 Scale	*Janet Storey*
Dolls' House Accessories, Fixtures and Fittings	*Andrea Barham*
Dolls' House Furniture: Easy-to-Make Projects in 1/12 Scale	
	Freida Gray
Dolls' House Makeovers	*Jean Nisbett*
Dolls' House Window Treatments	*Eve Harwood*
Edwardian-Style Hand-Knitted Fashion for 1/12 Scale Dolls	
	Yvonne Wakefield

MAGAZINES

WOODTURNING ◆ WOODCARVING ◆ FURNITURE & CABINETMAKING

THE ROUTER ◆ NEW WOODWORKING ◆ THE DOLLS' HOUSE MAGAZINE

OUTDOOR PHOTOGRAPHY ◆ BLACK & WHITE PHOTOGRAPHY

MACHINE KNITTING NEWS ◆ KNITTING

GUILD OF MASTER CRAFTSMEN NEWS

The above represents a full list of all titles currently published or scheduled to be published.
All are available direct from the Publishers or through bookshops, newsagents and specialist retailers.
To place an order, or to obtain a complete catalogue, contact:

GMC Publications,
Castle Place, 166 High Street, Lewes, East Sussex BN7 1XU United Kingdom
Tel: 01273 488005 Fax: 01273 402866
E-mail: pubs@thegmcgroup.com
Website: www.gmcbooks.com
Orders by credit card are accepted